Never Stop Learning

The Lessons Learned Series

Learn how the most accomplished leaders from around the globe have tackled their toughest challenges in the Harvard Business Press *Lessons Learned* series.

Concise and engaging, each volume in this series offers fourteen insightful essays by top leaders in industry, the public sector, and academia on the most pressing issues they've faced. The *Lessons Learned* series also offers all of the lessons in their original video format, free bonus videos, and other exclusive features on the 50 Lessons companion Web site: **www.50lessons.com/learning.**

Both in print and online, *Lessons Learned* contributors share surprisingly personal and insightful anecdotes and offer authoritative and practical advice drawn from their years of hard-won experience.

A crucial resource for today's busy executive, *Lessons Learned* gives you instant access to the wisdom and expertise of the world's most talented leaders.

Other books in the series:

Never Stop Learning

LES50NS

www.50lessons.com/learning

Boston, Massachusetts

Printed in the United States of America
14 13 12 11 10 5 4 3 2 1

Library of Congress Cataloging-in-Publication Data

Never stop learning.
     p. cm. — (Lessons learned)
   ISBN 978-1-4221-3990-5 (pbk. : alk. paper)
  1. Employees—Training of.   2. Organizational
learning.
   HF5549.5.T7N45 2010
   658.3'124—dc22

                                        2010008139

In partnership with 50 Lessons, a leading provider of digital media content, Harvard Business Press is pleased to offer *Lessons Learned*, a book series that showcases the trusted voices of the world's most experienced leaders. Through the power of personal storytelling, each book in this series presents the accumulated wisdom of some of the world's best-known experts and offers insights into how these individuals think, approach new challenges, and use hard-won lessons from experience to shape their leadership philosophies. Organized thematically according to the topics at the top of managers' agendas—leadership, change management, entrepreneurship, innovation, and strategy, to name a few—each book draws from 50 Lessons' extensive video library of interviews with CEOs and other thought leaders. Here, the world's leading senior

A Note from the Publisher

executives, academics, and business thinkers speak directly and candidly about their triumphs and defeats. Taken together, these powerful stories offer the advice you'll need to take on tomorrow's challenges.

As you read this book, we encourage you to visit **www.50lessons.com/learning** to view videos of these lessons as well as additional bonus material on this topic. You'll find not only new ways of looking at the world, but also the tried-and-true advice you need to illuminate the path forward.

⊰ CONTENTS ⊱

Contents

Contents

"How have you helped me learn lately?" may well be the question of a new generation of Millennial workers. In a survey of 2,200 global working professionals, conducted on behalf of the book, *The 2020 Workplace*, Millennial workers share how they seek out employers who invest in learning and development. The way your organization addresses its commitment to learning and development may well be your competitive advantage in the global marketplace.

In *Never Stop Learning*, senior executives charged with developing and promoting continuous learning share firsthand accounts of how they develop strategies to ensure executives never stop learning. You will get a peek into the future of learning and see how these practitioners are reinventing, reimagining, and rethinking corporate learning to be:

Action learning: Senior executives are intent that learning must not only be aligned to business priorities but also action-oriented and focused on real business issues. Toshiba is one example where high potential managers come together in competing teams to analyze a business issue and then propose a solution that has the potential to generate growth for the organization. The result for Toshiba has been profound: one project was funded with corporate seed money and later became one of the top six company initiatives.

Wearable and mobile: Learning is becoming both wearable and highly mobile at a growing number of companies. Watson Pharmaceutical is one company whose vision is to equip each salesperson with an iPhone and an app for Watson University, the company's corporate university. From there, salespeople can access online learning courses, hear podcasts, read documents, and view presentations, all while on the road visiting clients.

Engaging: If learning is to stick, it must be engaging to adult learners. Sun Microsystems is a model for how to use simulations and games to train senior directors in a new strategy for the company. Rather than have the directors sit through a class on a new corporate strategy, Sun Learning Services developed an engaging experiential learning exercise where the senior directors experienced the new strategy and, as a team, practiced how the strategy could drive business results.

Innovative: When you read elsewhere about learning in the U.S. Army you may focus on its traditional programs that are outcome based. But U.S. Army learning is a hotbed of experimentation in using the latest social media tools such as blogs, wikis, and even Facebook groups to promote greater collaboration and knowledge sharing across the globe.

Collaborative: As organizations become more complex, more global, and more virtual, there is a greater need to increase collaboration between employees to solve problems, suggest new ideas, and communicate across time zones. In this networked enterprise, corporate learning at companies

Foreword

such as Steelcase, Cisco, and GE Healthcare is moving from an individual experience to one that is networked and encourages shared learning experiences.

As you read these stories from senior executives—some of whom are chief learning officers while others are C-level executives—you will be struck by just how much the workplace is changing, moving from the Information Age to the Collaboration Age; one where employees work, communicate, and learn in ways that may be to some unimaginable. The workplace of iPhones, iPads, video games, business simulations, and corporate social networks will change forever how and where we learn. Our job is to ensure we never stop learning.

Jeanne C. Meister

Coauthor, *The 2020 Workplace: How Innovative Companies Attract, Develop & Keep Tomorrow's Employees Today*
Founding Partner, Future Workplace

How Learning Has Evolved

Dan Parisi

*Executive Vice President and
Senior Partner, BTS USA*

I DID SOME RESEARCH recently and the Western civilization's standard approach to adult learning started at monasteries in Europe. In between crafting fine ales and champagne, monks would spend many, many hours a day in what was called the lecture and scribe method. There would be an abbot in a monastery who would stand up in front of the room reading from an old text and the monks would literally scribe the lecture word-for-word. This lecture-scribe model became standardized and spread through universities in Europe.

Now research shows that lecture isn't very effective. In fact, if you listen to a lecture and you're asked about what you heard in the lecture the next day, you retain about 5 to 10 percent of it. The interesting thing is that this paradigm lasted for four hundred years. It's still around today, but it took four hundred years for the next innovation in adult learning to hit. Christopher Columbus Langdell at the Harvard Law School in 1890 introduces the concept of a case study. What a case study does is bring dialogue; it brings a richer dialogue into the classroom because you're working with a real-world example. A case study, by definition, is an accurate historical summary of a story that people can then discuss and learn from. Already it's a step ahead of lecture because lecture was kind of a one-way approach.

How Learning Has Evolved

So in 1890 the case study is adopted at Harvard Law School and spreads through professional services schools, medical universities, and business schools.

In adult learning in a corporate setting there's been basically very little innovation around the delivery or the process of learning until the adoption of simulations hits the business environment. Before I get to business simulations, let's step back. Some of the first simulations happened at the U.S. military in the 1930s. The problem was young pilots were dying frequently and planes and equipment were being destroyed. So they were losing assets and they were losing people at an alarming rate as the aviation industry was beginning to take off.

An inventive guy comes along. He introduces the idea of a flight simulator to the U.S. Air Force and they were very skeptical, but he put together this cockpit; a very rudimentary cockpit with dials and knobs and levers that somehow simulated the plane and simulated important things like lift and drag and speed, and he put people through stress tests in the cockpit to see how they would react under emergencies and learn a new plane's controls. Well, this becomes a very successful approach. It saves lives and it saves equipment. This idea—called experiential learning—increases aptitude much more quickly than lecture or even case study. It allows practice in a safe environment. It's a learning that's visceral just as much as it is intellectual.

Some of the current innovations that we're working on today in providing business simulation experiences to major corporate clients involve the idea of combining both the hard business skills— understanding strategy in business models and key performance objectives—with some of the softer behavioral leadership skills. A lot of our cutting-edge clients are using our simulations as behavioral laboratories.

So on one hand, the simulation is cap- turing all the business model drivers and the stuff that makes the CFO excited around business performance and objectives and metrics. We're world-class at capturing that in a custom way to reflect our client's business. On the other hand, we'll work sometimes with internal client partners or external partners to create a behavioral laboratory where industrial psychologists will observe the leaders in the simulation to give them feedback on how they're performing on the behavioral side. These experiences could be three, four, five days long; totally customized to the client; often CEO-sponsored or executive-sponsored; and we're tackling both what I call, right and left brain issues, which are the business performance as well as the leadership behaviors needed.

If you're a chief learning officer and you're thinking about engaging executives on content like strategy and business performance and leadership, I really recommend that you think a little harder before you use lectures or even case studies. I'm convinced—and I've seen it in action so many times—that simulations or experiential learning are really the most powerful way to connect with an executive audience; especially if the simulations are in the context of being realistic, relevant, and highly applicable to the job.

TAKEAWAYS

- Experiential learning increases aptitude much more quickly than lectures or case studies.

- Experiential learning includes visceral as well as intellectual learning and can be practiced in a safe environment.

- It is possible to target the acquisition of both hard analytical and soft behavioral skills within the same business simulation.

How Learning Has Evolved

⫷ Simulations or experiential learning
are the most powerful way to connect
with an executive audience; especially
if the simulations are realistic, relevant, and applicable to the job.

How Social Networking Sites Incentivize Learning

Karen Kocher

Chief Learning Officer, CIGNA Corporation

IN CORPORATE LEARNING, we have responsibility for internal employee learning and then also all of the learning for the external stakeholders that we think are most valuable to delivering on our strategy. As an example: because we're a health service company, we do a lot of work with health-care professionals and with producers and others that either sell or then deliver our various health services.

We've recently launched what we call Learn 4 Your Health. And Learn 4 Your Health is primarily focused externally. The goal of the learning initiative is to improve the health and the overall health management ability of the individuals that we serve. It's a very integrated solution. It takes into consideration social networking, so we have Facebook presence, MySpace, Flickr, Twitter, et cetera, as part of the solution. We also have a corporate social responsibility component; meaning that, for every question you get correct related to health, CIGNA donates a day's worth of clean drinking water to a Third World student. Lastly, we have avatar-based learning modules that are part of the solution.

Our goal is, A, attract your attention, courtesy of social networking; B, get you to be really, really interested in knowing more about health, courtesy of the questions—getting them right and donating the clean drinking water—and then lastly, for the point in time where you realize that maybe you'd benefit from additional knowledge around health, to then provide you with these avatar-based learning nuggets, which are highly interactive and engaging. We're finding that people really are gravitating to them.

However, what we learned is that, as much as we believe in health and that other people should take it seriously, people don't. So this year we offered an incentive component. For every program you complete, we offer you an incentive. It could be a coupon to Ruby Tuesday's or something like that. Whether we like it or not, you have to incentivize people to pay attention to their health and to learn more about health. So that was an interesting lesson. I think that's the same thing with employees in a lot of cases. It isn't enough to simply say we're offering the resources or the programs or connection to other people. There really has to be some type of a motivator for people, or an incentive.

For this particular initiative, the success measures were how many courses or activities people participated in, and then the amount of time they actually spent participating. We wish there were some way to correlate it back to whether or not somebody really has improved health or changed their behaviors related to health. But for right now, we've at least gotten to a point that we've got 3.6 courses being taken, on average, per person. Considering you're talking to just the general public, nobody we have any real control over, we thought that was pretty impressive. Per program, they're spending about six and a half minutes. The modules were made to be five-minute modules. So what we think that shows is that people are taking it slowly enough that they're really interested in learning the content, not just whipping through it in order to get to the end and get the incentive.

Never Stop Learning

The second thing that we learned was a very painful lesson. This year, we put our Facebook page out there. Last year we had it more as a fan page, so people could simply read about us. And it did motivate a lot of people to come look at our programs. This year, we said, "You know what? We're going to be really, really social networking savvy, and we're going to offer the bidirectional—Right, you talk to us, we'll talk back to you." So we opened it up. Unfortunately, with health reform being as volatile as it is, in one day we received fourteen hundred of the most negative comments you have ever seen on our Facebook page; not related to CIGNA, per se, simply related to health and how vehemently opposed some people were to health reform, and of course how passionate or positive other people were.

We learned very quickly that although we thought of it as strictly a learning solution, it is far more than that when you go outside the walls of your company and make it part of the company strategy.

TAKEAWAYS

- Learning solutions that are relevant to the learning styles and preferences of their intended audiences are more likely to be successful.

- Incentives may be necessary to engage both internal and external con- stituents, particularly around changing behaviors.

- Initiatives that are widely available beyond the walls of your organization may become vehicles for unintended use and/or unexpected outcomes.

Experiential Learning That Aligns with Strategy

Karie Willyerd

Former Chief Learning Officer
Sun Microsystems, Inc.

IF YOU'RE REALLY GOING to be a
strategic organization, you have to be asking
in your mind as someone is talking to you,

Experiential Learning

"What is it that they really are asking for? What is it that they really want to see done?"

An example for us was when the head of HR said, "We haven't trained directors in a long time"—I was a fairly new chief learning officer at Sun—"and so, could you create some training for directors?" That was the extent of the request.

My response could have been just a simple, "Well, it's easy to come up with training for directors." But what I stepped back and looked at was: what are some of the issues that are going on in the organization? And one of them was that we had a new CEO with a new strategic direction and he was frustrated that people didn't understand that strategic direction. We knew that from employee surveys. So we commissioned a team to work with the CEO and some of his staff to create a learning project that trained directors—and had a stealth mode of training VPs—around the strategy of the company by using a game. They played the game of run-the-company-for-a-week.

Never Stop Learning

What we were doing was perfectly aligning strategy to training because the training itself was on the strategy of the company. But it was not talking heads that were standing up and saying, "This is the strategy of the company." It was an experiential learning process. So while they were learning strategy, they were getting feedback on their skills as a leader. The VPs were getting feedback on their skills as coaches to the leaders. We were doing all kinds of tiered learning that was happening inside a single event.

When you design learning for adults inside organizations, the more that you can design a way for people to interact and contribute their own knowledge, the better. And not just have them do as we did in college, where you listen to a lecture and then regurgitate what you heard. That method of learning is going to be completely out the door for corporations. What's really going to be important is having games, simulations. We use games in our new hire

Experiential Learning

program. We use simulations in our executive development; having very complex interaction, so that people can see how all of these different variables fit together, because that's what real life is like. Real life is complex.

A lesson learned for me on aligning learning to the strategy of the organization, is that it's not going to be voiced to you in the question that comes to you. It's going to come disguised as another need. You always have to step back and be thinking "How do I help this request align to strategy?" Because the person coming to you is not going to be making that request. You've always got to have it as your motivator sitting in the background. You may not even have to say it out loud to them. It's just something that you have to look at as part of the learning organization, as part of being a chief learning officer; to have kind of a meta-thinking approach to every request that comes in: how do I align this to strategy?

TAKEAWAYS

- Real life is complex, so learning methods that recreate complex interactions, such as games and simulations, enable people to see how different variables fit together.

- When you design learning for adults inside organizations, the more that you can design a way for them to interact and contribute their own knowledge, the more engaged they will be.

- If an organization is going to be truly strategic, its learning leaders must find ways to align learning initiatives to business strategy.

Adopting Innovative Learning Tools

Wendell C. King

Dean of Academics, U.S. Army Command and General Staff College

I THINK THE MOST INTERESTING case study in the Army on innovation was one that came from a bottom-up example.

There were three company commanders commanding early in 2000, who were unhappy with their ability to gain information about doing their jobs. On their own, they started this thing they called company-commander.com—an Internet community of practice with other people who were commanding similar companies—so they could share the lessons learned and do a better job faster, more efficiently.

The original thought of the Army was that it was a security problem. First of all, that didn't turn out to be true. There was clear evidence that no secure information was being shared in the open network. The second thing was that this community grew so fast and the self-assessment from that community of its value was so obvious that there was no way to deny the value to, and the performance of, the officers who were involved in it as opposed to those who hadn't been engaged with it.

That evolved into these three people getting the job of setting up company-commander.com as a community practice for the Army, and it actually was moved to West Point. It was constituted in the faculty

Innovative Learning Tools

at West Point with these three young
people. That expanded into communities
of practice in many of the different specific
jobs that the young officers have to do. So
you have communities of practice for engineers, for adjutant generals' officers, for
infantrymen, and all of the different kinds
of jobs. It's also very specific to where you
are in your career. So company commanders will be engaging: lieutenants now have
these communities of practice: and they're
run by the education organizations now.
I think that shows the way you can learn
within an organization.

Our old solutions weren't working.
That was the other thing that really hit us
in the face. These company commanders
were being asked to do things that the
doctrine and approaches we had taught
them in the schoolhouse wouldn't make
them successful doing. So there had to be
a different kind of learning. This was
clearly filling that gap.

I think the biggest lesson learned for the
Army in this is, a new initiative needs to be

integrated in the overall learning approach.
It's not controlled within our Army
schoolhouse system, but it has to be connected to that. We have to collect that information. Where appropriate, it needs to be
part of the new way we teach and we learn.
And so again, it's that the Army is learning
from these systems rather than the Army
teaching these systems. That's probably our
biggest lesson learned.

TAKEAWAYS

- People will create and develop their
  own learning models if an organization cannot provide them.

- High rate of growth and improved
  performance are strong indications of
  a community's value to its members.

Innovative Learning Tools

⚔ When you ask people to do something
that your teaching models do not make
possible, a different kind of learning
may be required to fill the gap.

⚔ New learning approaches must be
connected to and integrated with
existing systems in order to benefit
and expand those existing systems.

Training People to Manage in an Increasingly Complex World

Marilyn Carlson Nelson

Chairman, Carlson Companies

WHEN MY DAD WAS RUNNING this company, especially when he started, he could go to one town and make a pitch and

An Increasingly Complex World

succeed, and go on to another with the same
pitch. He could make a pitch in one town,
learn from that, and go to the next one, and
he didn't have any reputational risk. If he
made a mistake in one town, he corrected it
but it didn't go on the Internet within five
minutes and make every other town aware.
Nowadays, the cost of being insensitive to
one of your stakeholders is so great that
the investment in the skill set to make these
complex decisions is more important
than ever.

The world is becoming so complex and
so interconnected and so flat—as we're
learning—that we have different implications to our decisions, different contexts
for decision making. I believe it's demand-
ing a different skill set or maybe even a
broader training. The business schools
have to move from the edge of the campus,
closer to the interior of the campus. The
business schools need to create next gen-
erations of case studies that have the
public policy institute or the public policy

school—and maybe even in today's world, theology and various schools—take a look at a case and ask: what are the implications, the human implications, the environmental implications, as well as the return on equity?

We happen to have a business school at the University of Minnesota, which is a very respected school—it's called the Carlson School of Business—and we are utilizing that faculty to train cross-cultural groups in next-generation thinking with case studies that we work on across our various geographies as well as our various industries. We have changed the course in such a way that we can bring more people from Asia, Europe, and Latin America to the course so that we get the geographic perspective and more philosophical input.

We are passionate now about moving people across our businesses so that they have exposures beyond their individual business. So, if the hotel people move to the travel business, they start to understand how the travel relates to community, how it

An Increasingly Complex World

relates to people's comfort, and gain a more experiential view of the next generation of products and services that we're going to build. As we move our legal experts across our various silos, they become more sensitive to environmental issues in cruises, for example, that might have a next generation impact on hotels. So we move our experts across fields to broaden their expertise and improve their contextual learning.

And of course, in today's world I think the complexity of the various faiths—how they're going to interface in the future and what kind of understanding we're going to have—is another element that we're going to need to introduce, in a much more explicit way, into our education about living together in global community. Because we are a microcosm, we are a global community at Carlson, we need to have those sensitivities and acknowledge those differences and that diversity as much within our context as we do within our world.

—◆◆—

TAKEAWAYS

—◆◆—

- ⚔ As the world becomes more compli-
  cated and interconnected, the
  implications and the contexts for
  learning, training, and decision
  making need to encompass more than
  return on investment.

- ⚔ Moving experts across various lines
  of business broadens their expertise,
  improves their contextual learning,
  and may position the organization
  to be more adaptive to future trends.

- ⚔ As company workforces become
  more global in nature, it becomes
  necessary to introduce learning that
  reflects different geographical,
  philosophical, and even religious
  perspectives.

Selecting, Training, and Supporting Sales Managers

Andris Zoltners

Professor of Marketing
Kellogg School of Management

I JUST FINISHED A GLOBAL
workshop with the sales leadership of a
company. Every year this organization

comes up with initiatives to try and improve the sales force. This year's initiative targeted the sales manager. How do we take that particular function and elevate it within the organization? Here's the reason for it: if I have a weak salesperson, for whatever reason, what I lose is one territory. If I have a weak manager, I lose the whole region.

It's startling how frequently organizations will admit that their management team isn't as good as they'd like it to be. What are some of the fundamental reasons? I see a couple. One is that we just don't put the right person in the job. The person who frequently gets the job is the individual who did the last job well. They were really good at sales; they blew it out; they were in the president's club. The feeling is that we should reward this individual and give them an opportunity to be a sales manager.

Well, there's a difference between the two jobs. If I'm in sales, it's about me. I'm the man; I'm making it happen. If I'm the manager, it's about the team; it's about you. I succeed through your success. So the two jobs are different. Michael Jordan was an amazing basketball player, but if he were a coach, one would have to ask, would he really be that good? You could see him tear off his shirt at the end of the game—big twenty-three comes out—and he wins the game.

That's the difference between the two jobs. What frequently happens is, we promote the person into the job and the individual who did the last job well is not necessarily the one who does the next job well. And it's a job that, once you go in and plateau, you're there forever. These sales managers frequently are in these jobs twenty, thirty, or forty years, so it's not a good idea.

The second thing that I discovered is that, whereas organizations have really good training programs for salespeople, they're less likely to have really good training for sales managers. The main reason is that you can't get scale. Managers are promoted randomly, whereas you bring in a lot of salespeople every year. Larger organizations will have manager-training programs, but there's not a whole lot of scale there, not a lot of good programs externally. It's really hard to make sure that the individual who gets promoted into that particular job actually gets the training that he needs.

This organization that I described did four things. The first thing is, it came up with selection. By the way, interviews are not necessarily the best technique for finding either salespeople or managers; we really have to put them through an assessment of some kind. This organization put together a really good assessment center, where they tested people for the skills that they needed for the new job. Subsequent to that they trained the individuals; this was global training. They also provided them with collateral with which they could succeed and the support systems internally. And even before they did all this, they defined the roles, the responsibilities, and the kind of profile of the individual that they thought would be successful in a job.

Those are probably four things we can do to elevate the job: number one, define the

job well; number two, hire against that
definition; number three, train the individuals; and number four, have resources for them to be successful
long-term.

TAKEAWAYS

- ✄ The skills and abilities that make individual contributors successful are not
  the same skills and abilities that make
  managers successful.

- ✄ In order to put the right person in the
  right job you must match skill sets to
  job function, not promote based on
  success in previous roles.

- ✄ Training needs that don't scale can be
  challenging to prioritize and to
  execute effectively.

Never Stop Learning

⚒ Four actions that will elevate a job are:
define the job well; hire against that
definition; train the individuals; and
provide resources for their long-term
success.

Effective Leaders Are Self-Aware

Bob Cancalosi

*Director of Leadership Development
and Culture, GE Healthcare*

FOUR OR FIVE YEARS BACK, I had an
opportunity to run a small organization,
about a $500 million business. One of my
best performers—I'll put him in the category
of being a high potential—wanted more than
anything to show how much he knew what
he was doing to the next level up in the

organization. I gave this individual an opportunity to do a complete business overview for one of our officers.

During his presentation, this particular individual paced back and forth across the room at least fifteen to twenty-five times in a thirty-minute presentation. When it was over, and under the theory of giving quick feedback, I pulled the employee aside and I said, "It was a really, really good presentation. But one thing I wanted to ask you: were you aware how many times you went back and forth across the room?"

And he looked at me with a very puzzled, quizzical look and said, "What do you mean, moved around? I was behind the podium the whole time."

And I said, "No you weren't." I said, "If you actually had a pedometer on, I'll bet you did a couple miles there."

So that was a big "Aha!" for that, my very best person; that he was not even aware of what was happening.

But that wasn't the defining moment. The defining moment for me was realizing,

Effective Leaders Are Self-Aware

if this was one of my best people and he was doing something that he couldn't see, what am I doing as a leader that I can't see? And I took that one more step into the organization. I looked at all the different senior leaders that I work with. I pondered, and said, "What are they doing that they can't see?" This whole thing came under a category called self-awareness, which is a big part of emotional intelligence, or emotional quotient. It was at that point I realized, people need help to be able to see what they can't see, to be more effective leaders.

When you look at different ways to make people aware of things that they can't see, I think there are a couple of critical ingredients that you have to have. One is, you really have to be authentic. And you have to care about giving the feedback. There's an old expression that I've heard, and I'm not even sure what the source is on it, but it goes something along the lines of, People don't care how much you know until they know how much you care. So when you are sharing some perspective to help someone become a more effective leader, you've got to come from an element of care. You also have to come from an element of being authentic; that what you're trying to do is in the best interest of helping them increase their leadership effectiveness.

TAKEAWAYS

- ⇥ People need help to identify what they can't see in themselves in order to be more effective leaders.

- ⇥ Self-awareness—a sense of how other people see and experience us—is a large part of emotional intelligence.

- ⇥ When making people aware of things they can't see in themselves, you should do so with authenticity and with care for their best interests.

—◆◆◆—

Fear and Doubt Are the Biggest Performance Inhibitors

Myles Downey

Founder and Managing Director
The School of Coaching

ONE OF THE LESSONS that I've learned in working with people is that the biggest inhibitor to performance is oneself: one's fear and one's doubt. Both of those things, fear and doubt, provide no earthly functions at all. I can give you an example of what I mean by this.

There was a gentleman named Bill whom I was working with some years back. He was very senior in a large retail bank in the U.K. He'd been ducking a conversation that we were due to have, which was how he was going to integrate two parts of that bank—significant parts of that bank—into one unit that he was then going to lead and manage. He simply, after two meetings, had not been having the conversation.

When I put that on the table, that we hadn't had the conversation, I could see his face drop and I said, "What's that about?"

His response was, "Well, I know I have to do it, but the problem is, I have only one idea, and it's not very good."

So I invited him to tell me what that idea was. He was right; it wasn't very good.

My response was, "What else could you do?"

Fear and Doubt

Bill kind of shuffled his feet a bit and kind of looked at me, and then he said, "Well, I told you, I have only one idea."

I said, "Yes, but what else could you do?"

At that point, he looked at me, he got a bit cross, and he said, "You don't understand. I'm not creative."

I heard myself ask, intuitively, "If you were creative, what would you do?"

Fortunately, Bill started laughing. And in the moment of his laughing, I was able to say, "Come on, just tell me one tiny little thing."

He did, and of course, out of that tiny little thing, something else grew.

The point about the story is that, it wasn't that Bill wasn't creative. It may have been true that he wasn't as creative as his brother or his sister or something, and had been told remorselessly through his life that he wasn't creative. That wasn't the truth. That was a self-imposed barrier. He has just as many billion neurons as anybody else and is capable of using them creatively.

Never Stop Learning

One of the issues that get in the way of people being more creative in the workplace is that our management cultures, despite all the work that we've done over the years, are still mostly about control. And that has precedence over creativity, or innovation, or even people standing up with a new idea about where to put the coffee machine. So the reflection that a leader or manager might do is about in what way are they getting in the way of their people?

The first thing to do, to make sure that that idea—that people get in their own way—has impact with others, is to simply, when people come to you, listen for two things. What's the potential here? See if you can hear it, and play it up, and acknowledge, and affirm it, and whatever else. On the other hand, listen for in what way is this person getting in their own way?

Sometimes, asking both those questions—what's the great idea here and how are you inhibiting it—can be enough to move that forward. And work with the leadership population so that, rather than suppress good ideas and rather than suppress people who are willing to try something, they listen for those things and allow them to happen. The only way this changes is if that attitude at the top of our organizations begins to shift.

TAKEAWAYS

- ⌁ The biggest inhibitor to performance is oneself: one's fear and one's doubt.

- ⌁ Self-imposed barriers may come from unexamined assumptions or unquestioned acceptance of external messages.

- ⌁ The idea that people get in their own way can have impact with others if you ask them, What is the great idea here and how are you inhibiting it?

Never Stop Learning

🔰 Leadership's attitude toward control and creativity has a powerful impact on whether an organization suppresses good ideas or listens to them.

Setting Your Own Learning Agenda

Victor Newman

Founder, KnowledgeWorks

THIS IS A HEAD AND HEART STORY. This is about listening to what's going on in your head and it's about listening to your heart so you're not the only lunatic in the room. In fact, if you're feeling fairly mad, someone else is feeling fairly mad, too. So, how do you work with that?

Never Stop Learning

This is a story that goes back to when intranets and portals were still wonderful beasts that people knew very little about. I managed to get invited to participate in a two-day intranet tour. What was interesting about this was that we were going to spend two days physically going from company to company, being shown these intranet Web sites, looking at the material and structure, and getting this wonderful death-by-PowerPoint-presentation from each company.

What was interesting about the group I was with was that we were all equally naive about intranets and we were all very interested.

Toward the end of the first day, we were beginning to become increasingly restive. It was as if we were going into the auditorium and getting this set-piece presentation on this big screen. We were beginning to look at each other and think that we didn't want any more of this. We thought we'd gotten enough from the first three presentations of the four on that day to start doing something different.

What was good about it was that, intuitively, we were beginning to build our own agenda. One of the things that I did was lead a mutiny among that group. It involved actually standing up and saying, "We have another day together. I think we have a great opportunity to build our own agenda. In other words, what is it we want to know more about? What kind of demonstrations do we want to see? What key questions do we have about investment and value and return on investment, especially? Perhaps if we could actually capture those questions and those issues, build an agenda, and e-mail it by three o'clock today to the four companies that we're going to visit tomorrow, we could have a presentation that actually met our needs."

So, I led that session and facilitated it with my ubiquitous Post-its. We grouped it and we brought it into themes. We allocated responsibility around the group for documenting that material for the next day and we e-mailed it away. When we arrived the next day, initially, they tried to give us the same stuff.

We said, "No, that was great, but could you now start answering our questions? Could you show us the following?"

And that was an absolutely wonderful feeling, to turn from being victims to some extent in that situation—that's a bit overstating it—but we changed from being recipients of a push approach to education, to a pull. And it was satisfactory in the sense that once we began to control our learning process, we became much more active. We began to listen better, and we began to know things.

I suppose it's one of the key things that I encourage people to do in workshops and in conferences; work out what your own agenda is as soon as possible and build your questions around that.

TAKEAWAYS

⚜ It may take some initial exposure to new information and new knowledge in order to focus on what you really want or need to know.

⚜ Learners who are able to control their learning process become more active, listen better, and find greater satisfaction in learning.

⚜ When attending workshops and conferences, work out your own agenda and build your questions around it, as soon as possible.

Move Out of Your Comfort Zone to Progress Your Career

Nick Adamo

Senior Vice President, U.S. Service Provider Sales
Cisco Systems, Inc.

I'VE BEEN BLESSED TO WORK for lots
of different leaders from whom I've learned
an awful lot. As I look back, they've all been
very, very different, with many different

skills. Quite honestly, I think one thing that I have a lot to be grateful for is, I was able to take some of the best from all of them and make it part of my style as I grew in my development.

When I think back, I was so anxious to move to the next role. In the company that I worked for at that time, the quickest way to do that was within the account that I worked within, so I continued to move up levels in that account. What I realize now and what I tell a lot of people today is, you are short-changing yourself if you're not taking on different roles and learning different parts of the business, because that really is how you grow significantly. You're not incrementing; you're growing in a whole new space, in a whole new set of dimensions.

I had been in the same industry and the same customer environment for eight-plus years. That was because of my goal to continue to get to the next level. One of my managers back then really forced me and said, "Yes, we have a next job for you here, but it's just not going to add to your 'scar tissue.'" He convinced me to go take a job outside in a whole different spot, a whole different discipline, something that I've never done before, in a whole different technology.

My first reaction was, "None of this fits my strengths. It has nothing to do with my current skills that I've developed over the past eight years."

He was right, and he said, "Yeah, that's right. That's why you need to do this."

I went into that and it meant having to learn all over again. It was having to create new muscle tissue, the muscle memory that you didn't have. You had to sit back and listen more than you thought you knew, because you didn't understand this as well as you previously did. You had to get comfortable with being uncomfortable, listen and learn, let other people help guide you, and trust in your ability to then make good business decisions.

All of that led me to my ongoing career development and led me not to be concerned about moving out of areas of comfort. I continue to move from certain parts of the business to whole new ones, and that growth, that constant learning, has been invigorating. It's been challenging—many times your hair's on fire—but it's been the part that I think has allowed me to continue to grow.

I would tell people today, move out of your comfort zone and do it sooner rather than later. Be comfortable that you're able to go and still be successful; and if you're not, then you have learned some great lessons, and you'll get better over time. Back then, that was not my line of thinking. That was not how I would have expected my career to evolve, and that's where I'm at today.

TAKEAWAYS

- You are shortchanging yourself if you don't take on different roles and learn different parts of a business, because significant growth comes from facing a whole new space, a whole new set of dimensions.

⚔ Get comfortable with being uncomfortable, listen and learn, let other people help guide you, and trust in your ability to then make good business decisions.

⚔ The challenge of going from what you know to what you don't know—that constant learning—can be invigorating.

⚔ Moving out of your comfort zone sooner rather than later will either give you the confidence that you can do something different and still be successful or teach you valuable lessons.

---●●●---

Learning from Mistakes

---●●●---

Domenico De Sole

Former President and CEO, Gucci Group

EVERYBODY MAKES MISTAKES. It doesn't matter how good you are; you can be a genius but you make mistakes. Every time a mistake is made you have to try to get something positive out of it and you don't do that by finding out who's done it. At the end of the day it's a mistake, and the management is in charge; the manager of the brand, the

CEO of the brand. Whoever has made the actual mistake, the CEO of the brand is responsible. Ultimately, I am responsible to the board and the shareholders.

I am convinced that the worst thing you can do in this situation is start running a search to find out who is the guilty party. That, at some point, becomes totally irrelevant; what's happened has happened and you cannot change it. Make sure that the person who has made a mistake understands that there was a mistake and, most important, understand at an organizational level why this occurred and why this mistake took place. Equally importantly, avoiding this search for the guilty party creates a culture of transparency within the company where people are not afraid; they don't need to cover up if a mistake is made; so be it, let's avoid making it again.

The negative impact is that it creates an organization in which there is a lack of transparency. People first of all either don't act properly because they're afraid of taking responsibility—which is really horrible for an organization—or secondly, they're more concerned about protecting themselves than doing what's best for the company. Certainly you cannot punish people because sometimes they make the wrong judgment. That happens; you cannot be right 100 percent of the time.

The issue is really to understand what the process is. It is a problem? Do you have the right process in place? What went wrong in the process? Very often it's not just one person who makes a mistake. Was the process set up in a way that allowed the organization to avoid the mistake, because they'd perceived the danger of going forward with certain decisions?

Having said that I really think it's important, in a calm, factual way, to understand the facts and learn why things went wrong and why a mistake was made. Something was done that people thought would turn out well and didn't, and I really believe that the key thing in this situation is to understand the facts and be sure that everybody involved understands why it happened, what went wrong, and how to avoid making the same mistake again.

TAKEAWAYS

⚔ Everybody makes mistakes. It doesn't matter how good you are; you can be a genius and still make mistakes.

⚔ Make sure that the person who has made a mistake understands that there was a mistake and, most importantly, understand at an organizational level why the mistake took place.

⚔ Searching for the guilty party when mistakes are made can create a culture where people are afraid to accept responsibility or where they're more concerned with protecting themselves

Learning from Mistakes

than with doing what's best for the company.

⧎ Very often it's not just one person who makes a mistake, so you may need to examine your processes and whether you have the right processes in place.

Align Corporate Learning with Strategy Setting

Terry Kristiansen

*International Manager of Education and
Development, Toshiba America Business Solutions*

ONE GREAT EXAMPLE that I have to talk
about, where we successfully aligned our
learning to achieve a business objective, was
something that we called the president's
challenge. The president's challenge was an

action learning program that was designed specifically because we had a business issue at hand. The business issue was that we were changing or we were adding to our existing growth strategy and we didn't really have a clear plan of what that was going to become. We just knew that we needed to do it.

The idea of putting an action learning team in place was something new that our education group brought to our president. Working in this way had the possibility of, fairly quickly, coming up with some great ideas for him to select from. And, hope upon hope, what if one could be selected to make a difference in the company? So he was game for that and aligned all the other executives around it. We'd never done it before. Could fourteen high-potential people from around the company really come together in teams, two competing teams, and come up with something that would be the new growth initiative for our company?

The process or the learning experience from that was so phenomenal. We had a three month period. We brought the participants in for one week where consultants provided a great program of assessments and background and looked at how they worked in teams. We also had executive sponsors for each team. That was key because it put more executives into the battlefield of action learning and allowed them to see the process in action and also contribute to that, to gain an ownership from it, and provide direction to the teams.

Three months later they come back for a week and they're kind of polishing up their presentations, doing a run-through of them and then finally they deliver them. Our executives, many of whom were just coming back from a trip from Japan, felt this was so important they literally got off the airplane from a twenty-two hour flight from Japan, listened to these presentations and were blown away by the depth to which this cross-functional team of people could go to understand the issues, investigate them, come up with their solution, and all in all, do a really outstanding job.

So it was tremendously successful and successful in that those ideas were put into action. It was a real business issue of the company that would take us in a new growth direction. One of the projects in particular was funded immediately with some seed money and both of them popped up on the top-six company initiatives. One of the initiatives actually landed us an account, the biggest account in the company's history. So we think we had a tremendously successful program run that is still delivering results today.

TAKEAWAYS

⧢ Action learning programs can provide the ideas and the processes for expanding a company's existing growth strategy in new directions.

Never Stop Learning

⚛ Executive sponsorship is critical to the success of learning initiatives by engaging leaders as stakeholders in program outcomes and by providing leaders the means to contribute support and direction to participants.

⚛ With the right support and preparation, a cross-functional team of people has the potential to understand business issues, investigate them, determine solutions, and deliver long-term results.

Enable Continuous Learning

Jason Zeman

Associate Director, Sales Training and Development
Watson University

OUR VISION FOR WHAT CORPORATE
training and development will look like over
the next few years is more collaboration.
And what I mean by that is more of this
true virtual classroom although it won't

necessarily replace live one-on-one meetings; what we envision is more of a blend.

For example, one of the things we'd like to do is make sure everybody has an iPhone. And we'd like to be able to create an app on the iPhone called Watson U. From there, users could access a reprint center. They could access maybe a podcast that we just put out or maybe the marketing department just put out; versus listening to a voicemail they could be listening to a podcast.

We'd like to record physicians giving a presentation. Maybe it's on disease state. Maybe it's on health policy. Whatever the topic may be, giving our sales force more opportunities to learn continuously— whether it be throughout the day, the week, the month, their career—but different avenues versus just one that involves a computer, or one that requires them to fly somewhere.

One way to enable this continuous learning concept, especially in our industry, in the pharmaceutical industry, is to show people how easy it is to continuously develop themselves. Another is to give them very specific platforms to do so. So, you have a computer, you have an iPhone, and you just really focus on those two things. Because a majority of people, they can't multitask. If you give them too much, their defense mechanisms are going to go up. They're going to shut down and say, "This is too difficult. There's too much going on, there's too many ways to get this information."

Whatever we set out to do, it really has to be streamlined. And we recognize that.

TAKEAWAYS

- Future workforces will enjoy more opportunities to learn continuously— whether throughout the day, the week, the month, or their careers—through different avenues.

Never Stop Learning

- ⚔ One way to enable continuous learning is to make it easy for people to develop themselves by giving them very specific platforms with which to do so.

- ⚔ Streamlining their options makes it easier for people to choose which platforms to use and which information to access.

Transform Learning into Performance

George Wolfe

*Former Vice President, Global Learning and
Development, Steelcase, Inc.*

WE BELIEVE IN OUR COMPANY,
Steelcase, that in 2020 our learning
organization certainly will be different than
what it is today. But there are several "givens"
because we're already on this journey.

Never Stop Learning

We will have already figured out how to be able to bring learning to our workforce just in time. Whatever technology, whatever requirements are there, we'll have that figured out because we're well on our way already.

The other given regards the whole issue around multi-generational workforce. We'll have this all figured out. There are experts in the field figuring it out and we're on that journey too. We will be able to offer different types of learning capabilities, in different ways, so that the individual can choose and select the type of way she prefers to learn.

We will definitely have figured out the capability of transforming learning into performance because that's what we're all about today, and we are making giant strides at our corporate university to bring value to our organization through performance; individual performance, which ultimately impacts organizational performance.

So 2020, to me, means those are givens.

What is still a challenge for us—it's our aspiration by 2020—is that, any time a

Transform Learning into Performance

leader in our organization; senior leader, mid-leader, any leader in the organization, comes forward with a particular initiative, whether that be a form of strategy, initiative around a new product, a new service, what-ever that capability, that new idea is, the thing that they do, number one, is to bring in the university upstream. Because they will realize by 2020 that change management—being able to get our human capital ready for that launch, for that initiative—will become key to the success.

Once we know what we want to do, what the next big idea is, we must also be able to focus in on a change management action plan that identifies who are the stakeholders here, who is this going to touch, and then identify, basically, from those whom it touches, how do we get them ready so that they can be the best they can be, prior to the actual launch.

We have a group of talented people within our university called performance consul-tants. They're engaging with leaders all the time to find out what their business needs are. One of the first things that we do is use a process called the Gilbert's Grid, sometimes called the Gilbert's Performance Engineering Model. We know that if an initiative is launched, there are key things that will interfere with performance and the success of a launch. By using the lens, up front, of the Gilbert's performance grid, our performance consultants can clearly set expectations of the employee. What is the expectation? What do they need to do? What is their role in this launch, and what are the processes and the tools to support them in that launch? What are the incentives and the award systems if they do exemplary work in making the launch successful? Is there a payoff or recognition? What are the skills and knowledge and processes individuals need to know in order to make this an effective, successful launch?

If we get this right *upstream*, before the launch takes place, we will be much, much more successful in terms of bringing the business results that our learning organization is all about.

TAKEAWAYS

- ⚔ Preparing human capital to manage change is the most critical aspect of successfully launching new business initiatives.

- ⚔ It is possible to anticipate and forestall the key issues that will interfere with performance and the success of a new initiative's launch.

- ⚔ A successful change management action plan identifies in advance of the change who the stakeholders are and how you prepare them to be the best they can be.

Never Stop Learning

⚔ If you can identify and put in place the necessary components before a new business launch takes place, you will be much more successful in achieving the business results that learning organizations enable.

⊰ ABOUT THE ⊱
CONTRIBUTORS

Nick Adamo is Senior Vice President for Cisco Systems Service Provider business in the United States. In this role, he drives Cisco's overall relationship, investment, and growth strategy in the ILEC (incumbent local exchange carriers)/RBOC, cable, mobile wireless, emerging carriers, and IXC markets. He leads a team of more than one thousand people and has revenue responsibility in excess of $4 billion annually.

Prior to his current role, Mr. Adamo was Vice President of the U.S. ILEC market and responsible for the company strategy and overall business relationships with the largest ILECs. Mr. Adamo previously held key positions in the enterprise market for Cisco, including the position of Vice President of the Northeast Area.

Additionally, Mr. Adamo was Operations Director of the Global Finance Operation for Cisco Systems in New York City, where he managed the global relationship of Cisco's largest banking, brokerage, and market-data customers in New York City.

Before joining Cisco in July 1995 as an account executive supporting Merrill Lynch, Mr. Adamo spent eleven years with IBM in sales and sales management assignments in the finance industry.

Mr. Adamo is Cisco's Board representative to Alliance for Telecommunication's Industry Solutions (ATIS) and currently serves as Second Vice Chairman. ATIS is a U.S. body committed to rapidly developing and promoting technical and operations standards for the communications and related information technologies industry.

Mr. Adamo is a member of the Board of Inwood House, a not-for-profit organization designed to raise money and awareness of the growing problem of pregnancy among high-risk teens in the New York City area. He was also Chair of Inwood House's first Corporate Advisory Board.

Bob Cancalosi is Chief Learning Officer for GE Healthcare (formerly GE Medical Systems) and is responsible for leadership, learning, and development of approximately 47,000 employees worldwide. GE Healthcare provides transformational medical technologies and services.

In his current role, Mr. Cancalosi leads a team of global leadership and development directors who design and deliver more than thirty specialized leadership development programs for GE Healthcare in thirty-two countries. He leads Global L&D, with responsibility for learning strategy and program implementation of new employee orientations, executive training programs, professional skills training, and specialty training events designed to tackle key business challenges. His current responsibilities also include leading GE Healthcare's global cultural transformation by identifying and implementing new competencies to drive growth in GE Healthcare's new organizational structure.

Since coming to GE Healthcare in 2000, Mr. Cancalosi has been in a multitude of general manager roles. Prior to that, he spent fourteen years with GE Plastics. He has more than ten years of sales and marketing experience and four years experience in quality control organization.

Mr. Cancalosi holds both a BBA and an MBA from St. Bonaventure University in New York. He is a certified Six Sigma Black Belt and Master Black Belt. In 2001, he was recognized as the GE Medical Systems "Leader of the Year," and in 2006 he was presented with the GE Healthcare President's Award for his work on creating a world-class culture for leadership development in GE. As a Leadership Development Expert for GE Healthcare, he conducts fifteen to twenty advanced leadership sessions a year across the GE organization at local universities and in the professional community. Additionally, he has personally mentored more than sixty people during his career so far.

Marilyn Carlson Nelson is the Chairman of Carlson Companies, the parent corporation of a global group of integrated companies specializing in business and leisure travel, hotel, restaurant, cruise, and marketing services. She began working with Carlson Companies in 1968. In March of 1998, she was named President and Chief Executive Officer. In addition, she took on chairmanship in 1999.

Though she stepped down as CEO in 2008, Ms. Carlson Nelson remains Chairman of Carlson Companies. In this role she leads one of the largest privately held companies in the United States. In 2002 Ms. Carlson Nelson was appointed by President Bush to chair the National Women's Business Council, a position she held until 2005.

Ms. Carlson Nelson is a member of the International Business Council of the World Economic Forum, and in 2004 co-chaired the Forum's annual meeting in Davos, Switzerland. That same year, she was selected by *Forbes* magazine as one of the "World's 100 Most Powerful Women."

Ms. Carlson Nelson is on the boards of Exxon Mobil Corporation and the Mayo Clinic Foundation. Additionally, she is on the Board of Overseers of the Curtis L. Carlson School of Management at the University of Minnesota.

Domenico De Sole is the former President and CEO of Gucci Group.

Mr. De Sole moved from Italy to the United States in 1970, where he earned a masters degree from Harvard University and became a partner in the Washington law firm of Patton, Boggs & Blow. He joined Gucci in 1984 as CEO of Gucci America. He remained in New York until 1994, when he moved to Italy as the Group's Chief Operating Officer.

Mr. De Sole was appointed CEO in 1995, and at the end of that year led Gucci Group NV's listing on the New York and Amsterdam stock exchanges. In 1999 he successfully fought a hostile takeover bid, securing Gucci's independence as a basis for continued expansion, which has included the acquisition of Yves Saint Laurent, Alexander McQueen, and Stella McCartney.

Mr. De Sole left Gucci in 2004, the same year he joined the Board of Gap, Inc.

Mr. De Sole has also served as a director of Newell Rubbermaid since 2007 and of Telecom Italia since 2004. From 2001 to 2005 he was a member of the Board of Proctor & Gamble.

Myles Downey is the Founder and Managing Director of the School of Coaching in the United Kingdom, which he established in association with the Work Foundation (formerly the Industrial Society), with the aim of "developing great coaches who can transform the performance of individuals and teams in organizations." The school specializes in working with the leadership and management population to improve business performance.

Mr. Downey is recognized as one of the foremost coaches in Europe and has worked with some of the most successful organizations across most of Europe, North and South America, Asia, and in the CIS, and in a variety of businesses, from professional service firms, banking, manufacturing, oil and gas, brewing and distilling, retailing, construction, and information technology. The predominant part of his work is in coaching senior executives and leadership teams.

He is the author of *Effective Coaching: Lessons from the Coach's Coach*. He also contributed to *Coaching for Leadership Development* and to *The International Guide to Management Consultancy*. Articles published through the School of Coaching include "The Place of Coaching in the Line-Managers Role" and "Buying Executive Coaching." He has appeared twice on BBC Radio 4.

Mr. Downey studied architecture and practiced in Dublin. Then, having read *The Inner Game of Tennis*, by Tim Gallwey, he began to work as a coach, initially in sport and then in business. He moved to London and was a founding member of a small, successful consultancy, which the Economist Intelligence Unit acknowledged in 1993 and in 1995 as the leading provider of executive coaching in the United Kingdom. He left the company in 1995 to investigate a wider variety of approaches to maximizing learning and performance, and established the School of Coaching in 1997.

Wendell C. King is Dean of Academics at the U.S. Army Command and General Staff College, which has a 125-year tradition of educating military officers on national security and the art of war.

About the Contributors

Dr. King directs a college faculty of more than four hundred personnel, organized into five separate schools, all with the mission of developing Army leaders for service to the nation. The U.S. Army Command and General Staff College is renowned for the study of leadership, the conduct of land warfare, and the synchronization and applications of all elements of military power.

In 1972 Dr. King entered active duty as a sanitary engineer in the Medical Service Corps, serving as a project leader providing environmental consultative support to Army installations worldwide. His next assignment was as an engineer staff officer at HQ U.S. Army Europe, where he developed engineering solutions for air, water, and noise problems. He was next assigned as Project Manager and Assistant Division Commander for the design of the Johnston Island Chemical Agent Disposal Facility. He was the government contracting officer for $42 million in environmental services supporting military installations.

After returning to school, Dr. King was appointed Chief of Environmental Health Engineering Division, U.S. Army Environmental Hygiene Activity-West, supporting Army installations in a twenty-three-state area. In 1991 he deployed as the Officer in Charge of the Southwest Asia Health Risk Assessment Team, evaluating the health risks of troops who had served in the restoration of Kuwait. The same year, Dr. King was selected to be Academy Professor and Program Director of the

About the Contributors

Environmental Engineering Program at the United States Military Academy (USMA). He led the development of a fully accredited environmental engineering major for USMA.

Dr. King was assigned to the Army chief of staff's crisis action team for the Rwanda relief mission as the Medical Operations Planner in 1994. The following year, he was promoted to Professor of Environmental Engineering. In 1998 Congress approved his presidential nomination as Professor and Head of the Department of Geography and Environmental Engineering. Dr. King directed a faculty of thirty-three in educating cadets of the geographic and environmental sciences.

In 2000 Dr. King completed his MA in National Security and Strategic Studies at the Naval War College. Five years later, he was deployed to the Office of Military Cooperation to assist in the development of the new Afghanistan Military Academy.

Dr. King holds a BS in chemical engineering from Tennessee Technological University and an MS in civil engineering. He received a PhD in environmental engineering at the University of Tennessee. He has authored two books, his most recent being *Understanding International Environmental Security: A Strategic Military Perspective*, and published more than thirty journal articles and dozens of scientific reports.

Karen Kocher is the Chief Learning Officer for CIGNA, Inc., one of the largest health insurance providers in America. CIGNA has won multiple awards, including those for excellent customer service.

Ms. Kocher began her career in learning as the Manager of IT Education at insurance provider Aetna, Inc., and went on to become the Education Director, managing frontline employee computer competency education in addition to her focus on IT professionals. She has had P&L responsibility for each of the educational organizations she has managed and is consulted regularly regarding the strategies she uses to build and lead highly efficient, effective, and profitable education enterprises and teams.

She has also worked at IBM within the Mindspan Solutions organization and had the role of Global e-Learning Content Solutions Executive. In this role, Ms. Kocher worked to define e-learning strategies, solutions, and offerings. Prior to joining IBM Mindspan, she was the Offering Executive of Advanced and Emerging Technologies education within IBM Learning Services.

In her current role as Chief Learning Officer, Ms. Kocher is responsible for learning and development for employees as well as external audiences, including producers, providers, members, and employers. Prior to this, Ms. Kocher had responsibility for learning and development for the CIGNA Service Operations organization.

Ms. Kocher has more than fifteen years of experience managing learning organizations, public training centers, and corporate training departments. In addition to roles leading education organizations, her background includes technical and sales positions within the insurance and financial services industries.

Frequently recognized by the training industry, Ms. Kocher was presented with a *Service News* magazine award for being one of the most innovative IT service leaders of the year. She has served on a variety of boards, advisory groups, and councils including the Conference Board's Council on Learning, Development, and Organizational Performance; Telecommunications Industry Association (TIA) Advisory Board; Capital Community College Advisory Board; and the Bridgeport University Advisory Council.

Ms. Kocher often works with vendors such as Microsoft, IBM/Lotus, and others on focus group initiatives. She speaks regularly at major events on issues surrounding corporate learning and business management. She earned the prestigious Chartered Property Casualty Underwriter designation in 1995.

Terry Kristiansen is the International Manager of Education and Development at Toshiba America Business Solutions, which manages product planning, marketing, sales, service support, and distribution of copiers, facsimiles, multifunction printing products, network controllers, and toner product.

About the Contributors

Ms. Kristiansen began her career in elementary education, followed by ten years in administration for a highly successful national real estate investment company. Returning to her true passion— education—and combining it with strong firsthand experience of a successful sales organization, she now has the perfect job at Toshiba, which combines expertise in education, sales skills, administration, and management of teams of diverse people and skills.

At Toshiba she gained experience in international leadership and education and is currently responsible for a staff of education specialists delivering leadership and sales education to five different sales channels as well as to internal corporate management.

Ms. Kristiansen is currently Project Leader for the recently launched Enterprise-Wide Social Business Network initiative, which is seen as a major organizational tool for leveraging the knowledge and skills of the talented people at Toshiba America Business Solutions. The project includes research of best-in-class programs, survey of leaders, identification and selection of world-class consultants and launch to the internal community to deliver results in line with the strategic objectives of the company.

In addition, Ms. Kristiansen currently leads a project for onboarding new sales professionals, which is a completely new look and execution for onboarding, and incorporates a full, blended learning curriculum, leveraging the most current technology. The goal is for sales professionals to reach greater productivity earlier in their careers.

Ms. Kristiansen holds an MA in education from California State University, Fullerton.

Victor Newman is the founder of KnowledgeWorks.

From 2000 to 2004, Mr. Newman served as the Chief Learning Officer for Pfizer's Global R&D operation.

Mr. Newman then consulted in financial services, biopharmaceuticals, national innovation development strategies, manufacturing, and telecoms. He also set up successful collaborations involving entrepreneurs and small- to medium-sized enterprises.

Mr. Newman next went to the Open University Business School where he led the development of the life sciences MBA and is currently a visiting professor in knowledge and innovation management.

Mr. Newman is the author of *Made to Measure Problem Solving*. His *Knowledge Activist's Handbook* was recently cited as the best management book within the last ten years. Mr. Newman also co-developed the Innovation Cafe. He serves on advisory boards for several organizations and has contributed to the *Harvard Business Review*.

Mr. Newman is the inventor of several Knowledge Activist techniques, including BoxLogic,

Barefoot, Predator, Baton-Passing, K-Box, and Innovating Behavior Portfolio.

Dan Parisi is a BTS Partner and the Managing Director of BTS San Francisco, a respected partner in strategic change processes.

Mr. Parisi began his career at BTS USA in 1995 as a junior trainer and simulation facilitator. During his career at BTS, he has pioneered the application of customized business simulations for leading *Fortune* 500 clients such as Hewlett-Packard, Texas Instruments, Toyota, and others. He has personally facilitated the training of more than seven thousand, five hundred executives and managers using computer-based business simulations.

Mr. Parisi uses business simulations as a "behavioral laboratory" for executives to get feedback on their leadership and team effectiveness skills and their business skills. He is also responsible for product development simulations that teach managers and engineers the complex interdependencies and trade-offs of time/cost/performance that must be balanced in order to win in the high-tech market place.

Mr. Parisi is the coauthor of "Creating a Customer Centric Culture: Walking a Mile in the Customer's Shoes" at Texas Instruments and "Using Business Simulations for Executive Development." *Training* magazine named him one of the "10 Top Young Trainers in the U.S." for 2008. In 2007, he was selected by Marshall Goldsmith to join the

About the Contributors

Marshall Goldsmith "Distinguished Thought Leaders Library" as a result of his years of pioneering work in executive business acumen simulations.

Mr. Parisi received his undergraduate degree in economics and philosophy from SUNY Stony Brook, with magna cum laude distinction, and his MBA in finance from NYU.

Karie Willyerd is the former Chief Learning Officer for Sun Microsystems. Until her retirement in February 2010, she led the award-winning Sun Learning Services (SLS) organization, which provides Solaris, Java, and other Sun software training.

Ms. Willyerd began her learning career at publishing company Prentice Hall authoring training materials. She then began working as an instructional designer at an engineering training consultancy in the nuclear industry, which helped her move to Lockheed Martin Tactical Aircraft Systems, where she led the employee development function. She later worked in executive development at global food company H. J. Heinz.

Ms. Willyerd then moved to electronics manufacturer Solectron, where she held the position of Vice President and Chief Talent Officer. In this role she was responsible for worldwide executive development, organization development, global staffing, training and development, performance management, and mergers and acquisitions.

In 2005, Ms. Willyerd joined Sun. One of her primary roles was consolidating twelve separate training and research-oriented functions into one cohesive group. At Sun, she has spearheaded programs that make more learning available online in smaller packages of content. She has also driven a strategy to make learning accessible through different approach paths such as by role, by product, by solution, and by certification path.

In her last position, Ms. Willyerd was responsible for employee, customer, partner, and community learning. This included product and technical training, technical publications, skill development, library and research services, and business, sales, and services learning. Ms. Willyerd also directed the globalization group, which produces localized versions of Sun's products to widen demand for Sun solutions in regional markets.

Ms. Willyerd holds a master's degree in instructional and performance technology from Boise State University and a doctorate in management from Case Western Reserve University. She is a frequent speaker at professional events and is involved with a variety of industry, academic, and philanthropic organizations.

Ms. Willyerd is the coauthor of *The 2020 Workplace: How Companies Are Innovating and Using Social Media to Attract, Develop and Engage Employees* (2010), published by Harper Collins.

George Wolfe is the former Vice President of Global Learning and Development for Steelcase, Inc., which specializes in international work effectiveness knowledge, products, and services that enhance the quality of people's lives in work environments. He retired from Steelcase in 2009.

During the early part of his career, Mr. Wolfe served as a tenured professor and administrator in the state university systems of Wisconsin, Ohio, and Michigan. Following these tenures, he worked as a senior executive at Bob Evans Farms, Inc. and the American Hotel & Restaurant Association's Educational Institute in the affiliated fields of education, learning, and professional certification.

Mr. Wolfe joined Steelcase in 1995, when he was asked to create a learning infrastructure for the international division of Steelcase that would service the human resources and sales training needs of Steelcase and dealer employees in Latin America, Asia Pacific, and the Middle East. He was appointed Vice President for Steelcase's global corporate university in 2001. In this role Mr. Wolfe led a team whose responsibilities include developing premier learning and development programs, curriculum, and growth opportunities for Steelcase employees around the world, and managing the overall operations of the company's state-of-the art learning facility: the Steelcase University Learning Center.

Currently, Mr. Wolfe is an Executive Coach and Consultant with G. A. W. Impact Consulting. He is also featured as a keynote speaker, lecturer, and presenter for a series of national and international events.

About the Contributors

Mr. Wolfe holds a master's degree in education from the University of Akron and a PhD from the University of Utah. He is also a member of the American Association of Training and Development Benchmarking Forum and the Intelligence Committee for Chief Learning Officer Media, and a member of the Editorial Advisory board for *Talent Management* magazine. In 2006, Mr. Wolfe won the prestigious Gold Award in the Strategic Alignment category for organizations with more than ten thousand employees from *Chief Learning Officer* magazine.

Jason Zeman is Associate Director of Sales Training and Development at Watson Pharmaceuticals. The company is engaged in the development, manufacturing, marketing, and distribution of generic pharmaceuticals and specialized branded pharmaceutical products focused on urology, women's health, and nephrology.

Mr. Zeman entered the pharmaceutical industry in 2001 as a clinical sales representative in the women's health division of Watson Pharmaceuticals. He quickly advanced to the position of Senior Training Manager and then to Associate Director. He has led key projects that have changed the culture of Watson Pharmaceuticals' branded business.

Mr. Zeman is now focused on envisioning and implementing innovative ways to leverage Watson's blended learning technology with the marketing department's promotional plan and the training department's development curriculum.

Currently, Mr. Zeman is pursuing an MBA in executive pharmaceutical marketing from the Erivan K. Haub School of Business at St. Joseph's University. A member of Sigma Phi Epsilon, he already holds a BA in marketing from West Virginia University. He studied international business while abroad in Seville, Spain, at the Cross Cultural Center.

Mr. Zeman is an active member of the Society of Pharmaceuticals & Biotech Trainers (SPBT) and the American Society for Training & Development (ASTD).

Andris Zoltners is a Professor of Marketing at the Kellogg School of Management at Northwestern University, where he has been a member of the faculty for more than thirty years.

Prior to joining Northwestern, Dr. Zoltners was a member of the business school faculty at the University of Massachusetts. He received his PhD from Carnegie-Mellon University.

Dr. Zoltners has written more than forty academic articles and edited two books on marketing models. He is the coauthor of *The Complete Guide to Sales Force Incentive Compensation: How to Design and Implement Plans That Work, Sales Force Design for Strategic Advantage* and *The Complete Guide to Accelerating Sales Force Performance*.

In 1983 Dr. Zoltners cofounded ZS Associates, a global management consulting firm specializing

About the Contributors

in sales and marketing strategy, operations, and execution. ZS serves clients worldwide with offices in North America, Europe, and Asia. His areas of expertise are sales force strategy; sales force size, structure, and deployment; sales force compensation; and sales force effectiveness.

In 2005 Dr. Zoltners was inducted into the Chicago Entrepreneurship Hall of Fame.

⊰ ACKNOWLEDGMENTS ⊱

First and foremost, heartfelt thanks go to all of the executives who have candidly shared their hard-won experience and battle-tested insights for the *Lessons Learned* series.

Secondly, a special thanks to Jeanne Meister for providing her refreshing perspective on current learning trends in an exciting Foreword. Additional thanks to Jeanne and the CLO Innovation Network for their continued involvement with 50 Lessons. For more information about Jeanne Meister and the CLO Innovation Network, please visit www.newlearningplaybook.com and www.future workplace.com.

Angelia Herrin at Harvard Business Publishing consistently offered unwavering support, good humor, and counsel from the inception of this ambitious project.

Kathleen Carr, Brian Surette, and David Goehring provided invaluable editorial direction, perspective, and encouragement, particularly for this second series. Many thanks to the entire HBP team of designers, copy editors, and marketing professionals who helped bring this series to life.

Much appreciation goes to Jennifer Lynn and Christopher Benoît for research and diligent

Acknowledgments

attention to detail, and to Roberto de Vicq de Cumptich for his imaginative cover designs.

Finally, thanks to James MacKinnon and the entire 50 Lessons team for their time, effort, and steadfast support of this project.

THE LAST PAGE IS
ONLY THE BEGINNING

Watch Free *Lessons Learned*
Video Interviews and Get Additional Resources

You've just read first-hand accounts from the business
world's top leaders, but the learning doesn't have to
end there. 50 Lessons gives you access to:

**Exclusive videos featuring the leaders
profiled in this book**

**Practical advice for putting their
insights into action**

**Challenging questions that
extend your learning**

FREE ONLINE AT:
www.50lessons.com/learning